How to Build

a

Winning Team

Steven Galindo

How to Build a Winning Team

Copyright 2011 by Steven Galindo. All rights reserved. No portion of this manuscript may be copied electronically or otherwise without the expressed written consent of the author.

DEDICATION

To the leaders and mentors who pour out their knowledge every day into the lives of those around them and empower their students and family to go further and reach higher;

To the managers and supervisors who are trying to grow and develop into the leaders they desire to be;

To every boss I've ever had who tried to teach me something new and different, and to every boss who tried and failed. I learned from you all.

Leadership is action, not position.

~Donald H. McGannon

TABLE OF CONTENTS

Introduction – You have to *build* a team

1. What Does It Take To Build A Team?

A desire to win? Commitment to a goal? Do you have what it takes to build a team? Here are seven keys to successful team building you must have.

2. Traits of A Team Builder

Inspiring trust, clarifying objectives and addressing critical partners are just the beginning. Here are 10 traits of a successful team builder.

3. Builders vs. Killers

Who's #1? Big me -- little you. Manipulation vs. persuasion. Are people a means to an end or an end in themselves?

4. Team Mates Speak Out

How followers think about their leaders shows why some teams work and others don't.

5. Do You Build or Kill?

20 questions to ask (and answer honestly) to determine if you build up or tear down by what you do and say.

6. How Team Killers become Team Builders

Nine things must change in your personal evolution.

About the Author
Other Books by Steven Galindo
Acknowledgments

He that cannot obey cannot command.

~Benjamin Franklin

How to Build

a

Winning Team

The task of the leader is to get his people from where they are to where they have not been.

~Henry Kissinger

INTRODUCTION

You Have To *Build* Winning Teams

We had labored together as a group for six months in a valiant but failing effort to save the company. Our boss had approached us half a year before and told us the firm was in decline. We had to increase sales and cut the cost of production in order to survive the coming recession. We laid a few people off, cut some hours and salaries and raised our rates.

We spent several evenings and weekends at the office trying to discuss -- but usually arguing about -- what more we could do to make ends meet. As the weeks became months and months became quarters, it became apparent there were a few on the team who sincerely wished to do whatever needed to be done to fix the problem. Others fought turf wars and engaged in character assassination (during "meetings-before-the-meetings" with the boss) in a desperate effort to gut other departments and protect their own. Even after the boss would stress the importance of teamwork and unity, these men (departmental leaders with high salaries and lots of influence) would attack and slander others and coerce the boss into agreeing with their competing viewpoints.

On the day the boss laid me off he said, "I have waited for six months for you guys to work together as a team and it has not happened. I held back, not wanting to step in and take over, hoping you would come up with solutions that worked. But you're not a team. You never have been. You can't work together." With that summation, he decided I no longer fit into his program.

Had I been one of the turf warriors, one of the character assassins, one of the manipulators who whispered in his ear before meetings about how to cut expenses by closing out another department or at least firing the manager and replacing him with someone cheaper, I would have felt like I had fought and lost. But instead I felt like I had been led into the woods by my leader and executed. I had been one of the team players, encouraging the others to set aside their differences, lower their voices and come up with workable solutions. Now I was out -- and they were still employed. It wasn't about economics. I was the cheapest member of the team. It was about politics and friendships. It was about dirty pool and favoritism.

A team that can't work together lacks a unifying coach who knows how to lead. As my boss' words sank into my ear, "You all are not a team" a thought raced through my mind: "That's because you're not a team builder." And in a lightning flash of crystal clarity it hit me that without a team builder, there is no team. Without a builder, the team will go nowhere. The team's ability to perform well on a consistent basis is dependent on how well the team has been constructed, and who's coaching it.

Who chose the players? Who helps them blend their talents? Who develops unity and loyalty among them?

Do you believe these things happen on their own?

The mark of a real leader is one who takes a bad team and makes it better. They can take a decent team and make it great. They can take a great team and out-perform everyone else. But the leader does it in such a way so that you *want* to do well. You admire the leader, you like the team and you outshine others because it means something personal to you. It becomes a matter of pride to stick together and win together.

So-called leaders who bully you show their inability to build you. There are Team Builders and people who tear teams apart. I call them Team Killers. A high turnover rate and low morale among workers indicates a Team Killer is in charge. If his/her superiors cannot see that and make changes, then they deserve to lose -- and you deserve a better team to play for.

This ability to build a team means more sales and better production in business.

It means more victories and better play on a sports team.

It means tighter unity in your platoon and conquering in combat.

It means strong families making wise choices in the home.

It means unified congregations with loyal bonds in a church.

If you have a man or a woman who is a Team Builder, they are worth their weight in gold. They are worth more than you are probably paying them. If you have a Team Killer, you either need to retrain them or remove them quickly before they destroy your team.

Let's break it down piece by piece and see what the various components are that make up a Team Builder. We'll contrast those qualities with a Team Killer so you can easily identify the two. We'll examine how various people feel about working for the two types of bosses, and discover how a Team Killer can become a Team Builder.

You may be a leader struggling in some area. You may be a great second lieutenant or a strong supporter of a builder. You may be a second banana waiting for your chance to take the helm. Regardless of your current position, the following information will improve your leadership qualities and help you understand how your current leader is either helping or hurting you.

If you desire to be a leader, knowing how to build a winning team is essential to your success.

My sincere hope is that you will see yourself in the following text, and make changes where changes need to be made to improve how you work, play, serve and lead.

First, a Word about Managers and Builders

Do you know the difference between a Team Leader and a Team Builder? Although I may use the terms interchangeably they deserve separate and distinct studies.

There is a fundamental difference between a Team Leader and a Team Builder in reference to *outer growth*. By outer growth I am referring to growing in numbers or physical size. Generally, a leader is responsible for leading the team or unit to some mark of success. He/she may or may not have been present when the team was assembled. Therefore, they will not have had a vote in hand-picking the various members that comprise the team. A builder – on the other hand – is the entrepreneur or the coach who scouts the field for reliable players and selects the right people he/she thinks will do the job best.

In reference to *inner growth* (which is what this book is concerned with), leaders are not necessarily builders.

A leader (manager/parent) is responsible for:

- leading the team
- making sure it stays on track
- keeping advised of the progress made and
- counseling what to do to avoid crises or how to get out of them

A builder focuses on:

- developing good team play
- enhancing personal interaction

- strengthening the ties between the unit members and
- motivating them to excel individually and together

In short, Team Builders are good at:

- building synergy in a group
- building a sense of loyalty to the family that rewards unity, synchronicity and accountability

A Team Leader is in charge of directing what that group will do. But he/she will also have to manage the team. Because it is made up of people there are times when the system breaks down or starts to malfunction. How the leader corrects the problems is determined to a large degree by his/her ability to:

- properly diagnose the conflict
- develop a workable solution
- activate the revised plan and
- monitor the results

All of this requires the cooperation of the team around them. How they handle those people -- and how those people respond to their directives -- reveals whether they are Team Builders or not.

If you see a Team Leader that inspires trust and loyalty among the followers there is a good chance you are looking at a Team Builder. If the team is fragmented and engaged in turf wars with low morale and heartfelt hatred for the leader and other workers, a Team Killer is in charge. Those teams lose.

People are more easily led than driven.

~David Harold Fink

CHAPTER 1

What Does It Take To Build A Team?

7 Keys to Successful Team Building

In working with business managers and owners as a Human Resources professional as well as my experience in different ministry positions serving in various churches I have had the opportunity to work with different men and women in leadership positions. By observing how they act and react, how they speak to superiors, subordinates and partners, how they respond to praise and criticism, and how they deal with trouble I learned to identify certain traits or characteristics in strong and weak leaders. They shared good and bad traits, were at times brilliant and other times misguided, possessed magnificent self-discipline and occasionally lousy attitudes and frequently had marvelous insight into why a program worked or didn't but were terribly blind to their own short-comings. Listed below are seven essential qualities to building a strong, successful team.

1. A Desire To Win Coupled With The Understanding It Cannot Be Done Alone (The Competitor)

2. The Ability To Forge Strong Relationships (The Unifier)

3. Harnessing Group Talent (The Recognizer & Organizer)

4. Trusting Others & Capturing Their Trust (The Nurturer)

5. Total Commitment To A Common Goal (The Visionary)

6. Loyalty To The Cause And The Team (Commitment /Delegation)

7. Relentless Drive To Make Sure "We" Win (The Motivator)

1. **A desire to win coupled with the understanding it cannot be done alone. (The Competitor)**

I never met a coach who wanted to lose a game or a pastor who wanted to shrink his congregation. Every person I have ever met in a leadership position wants their team to be the biggest and best. Every manager wants his department to shine. Every coach wants to win the championship. Every pastor wants his church to be the best-attended in the community. Every entrepreneur sees his vision of a glorious corporation unfold before him. None of them want to come in second place.

All leaders want to win. Some are so driven by it they are willing to make any sacrifice to do it.

You know of business men and women who have lost marriages and families because they were sold out to the company they worked for and neglected their personal relationships. I spoke with a drama teacher once whose high school theater department had a winning history in competitions and was highly noted for its excellence. She averaged rehearsing her casts and crew 18 hours per week, increasing it to 30 hours per week leading up to opening night. She had plaques, trophies and ribbons galore adorning the hallway leading to her classroom and stage.

In a moment of complete candor, she admitted: "I think my commitment to theater probably cost me my marriage."

Every coach wants to win but most realize they cannot do it alone. After a terrible performance by a football team one Friday night, a high school coach was quoted in the newspaper as saying, "Don't be mad at me. I didn't throw a single pass, miss a single block or fumble once!" And it's true. It's not the coach on the sideline who loses the game. It's the players on the field. Sure, the coach holds some responsibility. He is supposed to prepare his team and develop a winning strategy. But the players must execute it effectively and work together to win.

There are few things we can do to succeed alone. Most of the time our efforts require the help of others. Even so called "self-made men" read books someone else wrote, attend classes someone else taught, wear clothes someone else made and drive vehicles others built. No man is an island.

Bosses know they need their employees pulling together to complete programs. Pastors know their congregation is vital to their success. Coaches need their players cooperating to win the game. And parents realize the importance of coordinating their children's efforts to avoid chaos and assure success.

2. **The ability to forge strong relationships (The Unifier)**

The key to any successful relationship comes down to trust. Do you trust your partner to do the right thing when you are not looking? Do you trust them to say the right thing and behave correctly? Do you trust them with your money, your family, your reputation? Obviously there must be different levels of trust. We trust policemen but not as much as we trust our family members. And we probably trust our spouses more than most family members.

If you are going to build a strong team, you've got to instill trust in your members. They have to trust you, you have to trust them and they have to trust one another. Without this key unifying ingredient, your structure is faulty from the beginning, and will ultimately, under pressure, crack and break.

A basketball player is reluctant to pass the ball if he does not believe his team mate will make the basket. By the same token, you would not hire anyone to work in your accounting department if you were not absolutely sure they were someone you could count on to handle your money appropriately.

From the beginning, the winning coach knows he has got to be transparent with his team if he expects them to be transparent with him. When you are open and honest with your group, it will encourage them to drop their guard and open up to you. Once they can open up to one another, trust will bloom and relationships will strengthen. Lone Rangers like isolation because they can protect themselves from being exposed or taken advantage of.

Lone Rangers make lousy Team Builders.

Team Builders by nature are strong and secure. They know who they are, what they are capable of and what they can and cannot do. When you weave openness, honesty, transparency into a group, relationships deepen and unity forms. When your team is unified, a "one for all and all for one" mentality sets in. That is when your team moves forward as an unstoppable force.

3. Harnessing group talent (The Recognizer and Organizer)

Everyone on your team has a talent that landed them there. They probably know how to do their job better than anyone else in the room. That unique knowledge makes them invaluable to the group. One of your jobs as a Team Builder is to:

(a) Recognize who has what gifts and skills and

(b) Organize the team so that each member gets to shine in their role

It doesn't make any sense to move a great second basemen behind home plate to catch for the team. Nor does it make sense to transfer your best salesman to production. Every person is uniquely gifted and talented. Some may know what their abilities are and some may not. Some may assume they have a certain set of skills they don't have. Team Builders get to know their people, discover what they do well (recognition), and then set them in positions to excel (organization).

4. Trusting others and capturing their trust (The Nurturer)

Team Builders have to be emotionally secure and intellectually confident. Otherwise, they will be inhibited by fear and chaos will ensue. Leaders that don't share information or who guard their secrets usually have a difficult time building trust and commitment into their fellow laborers because their employees don't trust them. It is the old sowing and reaping process: you reap out of relationships what you sow into them – trust for trust, mistrust for mistrust. The attitude becomes "if you are going to keep your secrets, then I am going to keep mine."

Part of the process of expanding your power and increasing influence is the ability to invest trust in others. In sharing power and

information with others, you empower them to think like leaders and thus empower yourself.

That is what they must become in order for the group to succeed. Insecure leaders who keep their secrets and keep their workers in the dark maintain their supremacy -- but at what cost? Unless everyone on the field is on the same page of the playbook, failure is inevitable.

5. Total commitment to a common goal (The Visionary)

There have been plenty of books published about leadership and casting vision. Obviously, if you want your group to accomplish a goal, they have to know what it is. You cannot expect them to figure it out on their own. If so, they will all have a slightly different picture of what you are shooting for. It is vital you spell out for them what ultimate success looks like. Then you have to show them the path that leads to it.

To get them to buy into the vision and own it for themselves, it will help if you allow them some input. The Team Builder is definitely the visionary of the group. But it doesn't hurt to allow others to add something that will help.

It is also very smart to ask them to poke holes in your plans. Ask them to ask hard questions that require research to answer. Too often we cook up an idea and fail to ask the right questions to make sure it is water-tight. I was in a meeting once where after a series of questions and answers were given, one intelligent advisor asked: "Now we need to ask – what questions *should* we have asked?"

You don't want robots who only respond to what they are told. You want thinkers to think for themselves. Independent thinkers who buy into your vision will help you modify and correct it as you go. Often, they can help you avoid pitfalls they've seen others make due to their experience elsewhere.

You should spell out the ultimate mission of the group so well that each and every member of your team can articulate it in their sleep. If they cannot, you either have not painted the picture clearly and often or else they weren't paying attention while you taught it to them.

6. Loyalty to the cause and the team (Commitment /Delegation)

The men and women in your group need to be just as committed and convinced of success as you are. You don't want to be the only dog pulling the sled. If they have a part in building or adjusting the vision, and are empowered to do their part to make it succeed, they will feel they are a key to victory. Achieving goals equates to success for them.

Obviously they must not only understand what is meant by succeeding in accomplishing the goal but they must also know their part in it. They should be able to articulate what the company's vision is, what their departmental goals are and also be able to explain personal goals they have set for themselves. Being committed to a cause is exposed in a number of ways:

- Are they willing to go out of their way to help a fellow team mate?
- Do their personal goals line up with what their department is doing?
- Do their departmental goals line up with the project (or company's) vision?
- How much time and effort do they spend coordinating their efforts with others?
- Do they build up, strengthen and encourage fellow team mates?
- Do they offer honest debate and hearty praise appropriately?

The Team Builder needs to know he/she has committed people around them who have a "whatever it takes" attitude to win. It is your responsibility as a leader of the group and its builder to delegate authority properly. Having the right people in place is essential to your victory. A strong leader will know what their members are contributing and whether they are in the right position.

7. **Relentless drive to assure "We" Win (The Motivator)**

A Team Builder is relentless in pursing excellence and victory. I heard a football coach say once: "If you play the best you can, and you all play together then you are victorious. I don't care what the final score is." Admittedly there are different definitions for success. Everybody wants to win. Be sure to make it a "team win". In other words, if we win, it is because we all pulled together and did our part to ensure success. Even actors in Hollywood know they had a lot of help starring in a film. That is why their acceptance speeches are so long at the Academy Awards. It should be the same with you as well. If your team receives a special commendation, and you get to receive it, let everyone know you had a lot of help, and you're accepting on behalf of the team. Truly, victory is almost always a team effort. Even singles tennis champions who win the prize at Wimbledon will acknowledge their coaches and trainers.

    I overheard a boss speaking to one of his subordinates. This gentleman was considering withdrawing from a special project the boss had assigned him to due to an inability to commit the proper time to its success. At one point, the boss clapped him on the shoulder and said, "Mike, I need you. I picked you because I know you can do it. I'm not sure we'll finish on time without you."

    Mike stayed on the team, and the project came in on time. Although he was taxed to the max with time and pressure constraints, Mike stayed and played for one simple reason. He told me: "When he told me he had hand-picked me and that he needed me, there was no way I could say 'No'."

    With that one statement and one gesture, the boss went from saying "I told you to do it and you will do it" to saying "I picked you and need you on my team." It proved to be irresistible to Mike, and I suspect those words will have a similar effect on your team mates too.

The very essence of leadership is its purpose. The purpose of leadership is to accomplish a task. That is what leadership does–and what it does is more important than what it is or how it works.

~Col. Dandridge M. Malone

CHAPTER 2

Traits of a Team Builder

The more you work around managers, entrepreneurs and leaders, the more you find certain qualities and traits in the good ones. The following is a list of characteristics I have distilled from my 30 years in the business world.

1. A Good Team Builder Inspires Trust in Their Team Mates

By now you probably realize how important it is for followers to trust their leaders. Our military spends many hours and lots of money instilling trust in young recruits. They do this because it is vitally essential that the young men and women of our armed forces have complete confidence in their superiors. Commanding officers have to know their soldiers, seamen, airmen and marines will follow their orders when told to do so. The recruits have to believe the orders they are being given are trustworthy and intelligent. The same applies to the field of sports. When a play is sent in, the quarterback has to have faith (trust) in the coach that it is the right play at the right time. There is no room for error or miscommunication. Nor is there room for a lack of faith in the call. Any hesitancy on a player's part could spell defeat for the team.

The same is true in business, in churches and in families. Those who lead -- whether they are managers, ministers or parents -- must earn and keep the trust of their followers (direct reports, congregation, children). You earn their trust by showing your commitment and resolve to see things through to completion, to perform well and expect the same of others. You earn their trust by seeing to their needs as well. Once they know you are capable and confident, they will trust you. When they feel a connection with you (when they see your humanity and friendliness) they will follow your lead. When they can count on you to be accurate, consistent, professional and dedicated to executing the game plan, their trust in you (and their belief in the vision) compels them to work harder.

2. A Strong Team Builder Leads By Example

Years ago I had the opportunity to work with a boss who was one of those "Do as I say, not as I do" kind of guys. You've probably met the type. He never came in early but he expected his workers to do so. He rarely stayed late but he had no qualms about asking (and telling) others to stay until their work was finished. He forbade them to visit and chat with one another while they worked but it was not unusual to see him slumped in his leather chair with his $100 shoes propped up on his desk as he chatted with a friend about their next golf game. The longer I worked with him the less I respected him. I found out from my fellow laborers the feeling was shared by other employees. Why did we universally dislike or disrespect him? I think it is because when we see someone behaving poorly but holding us to high standards, it reeks of hypocrisy. "Hypocrisy" is a Greek word basically meaning "actor". People who we deem as hypocrites are people who are pretending to be something they are not. They are playing a role and not being real, not being honest. No one respects a so-called "leader" who is a fake.

An effective Team Builder builds trust into his team; trust for him or her and trust in each other. Most people can't trust or respect someone who doesn't pull their own weight. If you are transparent, open and honest and lead by example in how you want them to conduct themselves and their business, they will trust, admire and follow you.

3. Effective Team Builders Empower Those Around Them

Control freaks and glory hogs make lousy Team Builders. No one wants to follow someone who takes credit for everything that works. These braggarts blame everyone else in the room when things fail to work. It comes back (once again) to inner security. Are you secure with who you are and what you do? If so, you will radiate that when you interact with others. If not, you will project your insecurities and fears onto everyone around you.

There is a certain amount of power leaders carry because they are in a leadership position. What you do with that power will either cause it to increase (as your direct reports RESPOND to you) or decrease (as your direct reports REACT to you).

You can build influence and grow authority or you can shrink and deflate it depending on how you handle people. Please be aware that at all times when you are in a position of authority you are being watched and judged. Most people do it subconsciously. But it is happening all the time. Your words, actions and attitude reveal a lot about you. Even the tone in your voice sends a message about how you feel.

It is essential you share power with others. If you win, make sure it is a "we won" and not an "I won". No one likes to do the grunt work and then be ignored when accolades are handed out. If you fake being genuine, honest or sympathetic your hypocrisy will show through. That revelation will erode your followers' confidence in you. If you hand out responsibility and reward good performances, you will draw people who want to work with you and perform well.

One of the best statements I ever heard was when a new boss said to me: "You don't work *for* me, you work *with* me. Let's build together." It was inspirational, encouraging and made me want to do my best for him.

4. Successful Team Builders Stay Fixed on the Goal

One of the first lessons I learned in Cub Scouts was the importance of being able to properly read a compass. We went camping as a group, and I and a few friends of mine got lost in the woods. Fortunately, I remembered our Scout Master saying,

"The compass always points true north. Orient yourself to that, and you can always find your way home." I had noticed we walked south and west away from our campground earlier in our hike. So by retracing our steps heading north and east, we found our way back.

    Team Builders are not only responsible for casting the vision for the team (defining what victory looks like) but also remaining focused on the goal. If anyone loses sight of what you're trying to accomplish, the Team Builder should redirect their efforts. If anyone is going to remain true and focused on the prize, it should be the Team Builder. You build solidarity and momentum by drilling your followers on what the objective is and how it is to be obtained.

    I spoke with a WW II vet who served as a sniper for the Army in Europe. He told me there was a German sniper in a bell tower in a small town in northern France. His sergeant gave him the command to "eliminate" the shooter. He wasn't given any backup, no plan of action and no supervision. His sergeant told him a column of infantry and artillery were coming, and they needed to pass through during the night. The sniper had till twilight to take the man out.

    The vet told me his opponent had a distinct advantage. He knew the layout of the town, he knew the American forces needed to pass through, and he could see further and clearer than the vet could. The vet had to sneak in, stay out of sight, find the best angle of the tower where the shooter was exposed and make his kill shot clean and quick. He was also working against the sun.

Slipping from house to house, down alleyways and using shrubs, hedges, trees and buildings, the soldier managed to wriggle into a small clearing two blocks away from the tower. The German shooter was cautious, knowing the Americans were at the edge of town and probably approaching. He had to have known they would send a killer to hunt him. Eventually, he urinated in a bottle and poured it out one side of the tower. That was when the vet sent him to his reward.

In relaying the story to me, he said: "There were a lot of things trying to crowd in on my mind. When would the tanks arrive? When would the sun set? Was there more than one sniper? What if he slipped away? I had to push all that away, and focus on the one thing I had to take care of that day: I had to find him and kill him. And I did."

Focusing on our objective with laser-like precision helps you avoid meaningless, fruitless ventures that take you away from the task at hand. Many things vie for our attention. What matters most is taking the next step closer to success.

5. Efficient Team Builders are Good at Clarifying Objectives

Since the vision is usually the product of the entrepreneur, it is his task to state and clarify the objective clearly. It is only as a unified team moves forward to converge on success will they be able to overcome obstacles and accomplish their cause. It is a good idea to have visual aids of what the goal is to remind and inspire the team members.

During the Gulf War of 1990, Colin Powell (who was then serving as Chairman of the Joint Chiefs of Staff) was briefing reporters on the war when he used the phrase "total victory".

One of the journalists asked, "How do you define total victory?"

General Powel replied: "When you see an American infantryman standing in downtown Baghdad, Iraq with an M-16 and there is no returning fire, you've achieved total victory."

When a leader clarifies the goal, it gives the team a sense of purpose and identifies the target they need to aim for.

6. Competent Team Builders Preach and Live Team Work

This goes back to an earlier point. Team Builders know they cannot achieve the success they desire on their own. It takes a team effort. Therefore -- realizing they need people surrounding them who can help them get the job done -- Team Builders not only rely on others to help but actively recruit others who specialize in areas they will need assistance in.

Walt Disney was giving some school kids a tour of Disney Studios. They neared the end of their trek, and he asked if they had any questions.

One little boy asked, "Are you the one that draws Mickey Mouse?"

Disney replied: "No. I hired an artist to draw him."

A little girl asked: "Do you do the voice of Donald Duck?"

Disney said, "No. I hired an actor to do the voices."

Another little boy said, "I bet you don't come up with the stories or write the music either, do you?"

Amused, Disney admitted: "No, I don't. I have writers and musicians who do that."

Exasperated, one of the girls said, "Then what exactly do you do around here?"

After some of his employees laughed quietly, Walt Disney confessed: "Well, actually not much really."

A competent Team Builder knows their weaknesses and hires people to do what they cannot. Part of empowering others is hiring people who have skills you don't have who will work with you to help achieve your goals. When we live and preach team work the team is unified to work together.

7. Wise Team Builders Don't Care Who Gets the Credit

Most endeavors worth trying require the talents and abilities of more than one person. Even a painter needs someone to help him copy his prints and market them for sale. Writers require an entire publishing company to get their books out to the public. Regardless of what industry you find yourself in, everyone sooner or later has to ask for help. As a company grows, more people will be needed for success. In time, some may come to the forefront due to special skills and gifts they bring. It is vital that the builder recognize who these people are, and make sure they receive the accolades they deserve.

Nurturing skills come into play in this area. It is important to stroke the race horses that are winning, and encourage the strugglers who are easy to overlook and forget. The one who gets your coffee and runs your errands wants as much positive reinforcement as the one who made the big sale or snagged the lucrative contract. The receptionist up front is just as vital to your company's image as the software developer who is a genius. Both are needed. Both want recognition. The Team Builder should not be afraid to hand out compliments when they are due. Knowing how to stroke egos and encourage others is an incredibly powerful gift to share. It really does not matter who gets credit for the "win" as long as it is understood that it took a team to pull it off.

I was pleasantly surprised when a young college quarterback was praised for his superior performance after an important conference game. Instead of bragging on his passing yardage and his number of pass completions, he said: "I have one of the best offensive lines in the country. Were it not for those five guys, and their blocking ability, I couldn't do anything."

Bravo! That is the unselfish spirit in a secure leader that makes others want to work for him.

When you are liberal in your praise and accolades and selfless when it comes to sharing credit, you motivate your team to work harder.

8. Smart Team Builders Know the "Team Win" is Everything

A thousand coaches have said it: "There is no 'I' in T-E-A-M." Teams that work together usually win the game. It is next to impossible for a group to accomplish anything of any significance if there is poor communication, infighting and low morale.

I used to work for a company owner who praised his achievers, slammed his strugglers, talked badly about managers to other managers and generally took credit for anything his guys did right. Needless to say, the management team was at each other's throats. They distrusted their boss, and failed to meet deadlines because they were reluctant to work together. Their tardiness and failures fueled his anger which he unloaded on his men. Subsequently, he perpetuated the problems in his company.

Team Builders know they must:

- build a vision their group can follow
- build morale so the team believes they can succeed
- build momentum that keeps the group on track and moving forward

This sounds like a lot of work – and it is. No

one ever said team building was easy. Part coach/part cheerleader, the Team Builder must work daily to unify the team and propel it forward. Glory-hogs and nay-sayers don't fit the profile. Their insecurities assure defeat. Why? Basically, they are too small for the job. To make it to the top, *everyone* needs to be pulling – and *everyone* deserves credit for success.

9. Mature Team Builders Address Disloyalty and Backbiting

Inevitably, you will have people on your team who do not enjoy working with you. There could be several reasons for this:

- team mates turn them off
- they are unhappy with their wages
- the project isn't challenging or glamorous
- they are unhappy with life, and they blame their jobs for it

Whatever the reason, you will on occasion encounter bad attitudes coming from your employees. These folks don't keep their feelings to themselves. They feel the need to speak with anyone who will listen to them about –

1. their buffoon of a boss
2. their paltry pay
3. their awful office
4. their creepy coworkers

5. how they can't wait to leave, and work elsewhere where they'll be treated fairly (i.e., paid more and put in charge.)

    No job is perfect. There will always be something we don't care for. If the complainers kept their feelings to themselves it would be a great day. Unfortunately, they find it impossible to do that. Therefore they tend to drift around your offices, spewing their nasty remarks and complaints to sympathetic ears. Most folks let it go in one ear and out the other. Some go home and fret about what they've heard but never say anything to anyone because they don't like confrontations. Then there are those who will take it and run with it, publishing complaints far and wide.

    Gossip is like a poison that spreads and infects the whole body if not dealt with quickly. It is up to the leader to address the rumors. It is best if it can be in a one-on-one situation with the complainer. This is one of the true tests of a Team Builder.

Can you confront co-workers with dignity and respect and remain professional while disciplining them?

    Employees who are disloyal to the company or backbiters who like to tear at others verbally need to be urged to keep their feelings to themselves or else they will find themselves working elsewhere. Their commitment should be evidenced not only by their showing up and collecting a paycheck but also by saying things that are encouraging, uplifting and team building. If they are incapable of doing so, they either need to quit, be fired or learn to shut their mouths.

I worked with an employer once who told me, "If they don't like working here, let's set them free (i.e., fire them) so they can go find happiness elsewhere."

It is not easy to confront a negative attitude. It is even harder to do so when your personal feelings have been hurt or insulted. Make sure you are cool, calm and collected when confronting and do it with grace and dignity. There is no need to lower yourself to hostility when dealing with a malcontent.

10. The Best Team Builders Stroke Team Players and Weed Out Nay-Sayers

People who perform well deserve to be recognized and compensated for their contributions. I'll invent an adage: "The more you stroke the racehorse, the faster she'll run." Hard workers work hard because:

(a) they want recognition and
(b) they want a raise or a bonus

If they have earned it and you give them one, they'll work harder. If they earn it and you fail to recognize their efforts or fail to compensate them adequately, they'll be demoralized, grow discontent and eventually seek new employment elsewhere. The best Team Builders know their people, can see who is producing and know how to encourage, inspire and motivate them to even greater success.

One of the areas where Team Builders and Team Managers part is how they handle those who are not producing as well as they could be. Most managers (typical leaders) will threaten poor performers with a loss of employment, a demotion, a transfer or a cut in pay if they do not start performing better. This may work in some cases. There are some employees who need a kick in the rear to be motivated to do what they are being paid for. However, not all laborers respond well to threats. In fact, sometimes a threat will have the opposite effect: instead of making them work harder or better it may instead demoralize them even further and spur them to look for work elsewhere. While some managers would see this as a good thing (losing a poor performer) in reality, it actually costs the company more money to lose a worker. If you do, you have to spend more time and money to hire and train their replacement. It might be cheaper in the long run to find a way to motivate the struggling worker to perform better.

I use the analogy of an older automobile. You may own an old car that has lots of mileage on it. It's leaking in some places, and breaks down every once in awhile. You may need to get a newer car but can you afford it? What do you do?

You baby the old car, taking as good care of it as possible. Yes, it would be easier to have a newer car sitting in your garage that doesn't have any problems. Your stress would diminish. Your enjoyment would increase. But the cost of a new one may be more expensive than taking care of your old one. You can certainly plan on buying a better car and save some money for it. But you may not be in a situation right now to make the financial commitment of purchasing either a new car or just a newer one with lower mileage.

The same holds true with people who work with you. While it is true that a new employee freshly hired and trained may be tempting – especially if you have an employee who has been there awhile and is not producing – but consider the cost of firing one and hiring the other. Consider what you've invested in your employee, and ask yourself: "Is it cheaper to fix this one? Or is it cheaper to terminate this one and hire a new one?"

Remember: someone has to train the new one. That takes the trainer away from their job. One of the number one complaints new employees make is the lack of training they receive when hired. It often leads to a poor performance rating and frustration for the new worker as well as the employer.

I understand the frustration you feel if you are paying someone a competitive wage, and their performance has dropped off significantly. A smart Team Builder will:

(1) sit down with them
(2) find out what is going on
(3) ask why their performance is off
(4) explain that a change must take place

Discuss their happiness with their job and co-workers. Is anything going on in their personal life that may be distracting them while they are at the office? How is their health? Major changes in their lives may impact their work performance. I am not advocating "touchy-feely" psychology. However, if you consider yourself someone who knows people and can lead them well then you should take the time out of your day to invest it personally in people who are trying to help the company succeed – and struggling.

Sometimes a pep talk is all it takes. Other times, you may need to set specific goals for them to achieve and give them a reasonable timetable for success. Their understanding must be that the goals must be met by the deadline or they will be put on probation which may lead to suspension or termination. Make sure they understand the timeline and the performance specs you seek. They need to know each step and what they must do to avoid termination and assure their continued employment. A Team Builder will take the time to go through this process because they value each player.

It is also important to make sure they know the ball is in their court. They can change their destiny one way or the other. It is up to them to improve. Making sure they have the tools, time and training to do so is up to you.

A warning should be sufficient to silence a negative, backbiting employee. Usually once they are aware that their boss has heard some of their statements, they tend to get quiet and focus on work. If their griping continues, they either need to be put on probation or fired for insubordination. This covers e-mails, text messages, personal blogs, postings to Facebook or Twitter, too. Griping, backbiting, complaining and whining is a cancer that infects everyone if it is not dealt with quickly.

As a Human Resources professional, I try everything in my power to salvage employees who jeopardize their careers. I never want to lose anyone because that means recruiting and training someone new who may or may not work out. There are people who will always find something to gripe about and will do so to anyone who will listen. If you have a constant complainer, action must be taken. A meeting is inevitable. It can either be instructional so they can change and keep their job or a confrontation that leads to a warning, suspension or termination. The morale of your remaining employees will go up when they see that:

    (a) the whiner has been dealt with, and
    (b) you care enough to weed out those who would rather complain than work.

Nearly all men can stand adversity, but if you want to test a man's character, give him power.

~Abraham Lincoln

CHAPTER 3

The Differences between a Team Builder and a Team Killer

There are major differences between team builders and team killers. The chart below illustrates a few. Review it and you may find some of your old bosses, current employers and maybe yourself, too if you are in a position of management.

Team Builders	Team Killers
build people up	tear people down
show concern for coworkers	do not care about others
share success with everyone	take credit for all success
secure and confident	insecure, lack confidence
share information with others	hoard data
harness team energy	dispel energy which invites entropy
respect coworkers	disrespect their team mates

Team Builders

Team Builders are caring individuals who aren't afraid to sympathize and even empathize with their employees. (I hesitate to use the word "employees" because most team builders see themselves as fellow players or coaches and do not adopt the standard superior-subordinate view.)

They respect themselves and therefore are able to respect others around them. They are not afraid to show admiration for their talented team mates.

Team builders are invested emotionally and professionally in their fellow workers – not just on the job and but in their lives as well. I worked once with a boss who knew which of his employees had special needs children, which were struggling in their marriages and was personally paying for the counseling of one of his employees and the employee's wife who had lost their son to cancer a year previously. The fact that he knew what was going on their lives, cared enough to remember it and be proactive in reaching out to them was impressive.

Because team builders tend to be very relational, their relationships with other people mean as much to them as the actual company mission itself. I am not referring to group hugs or sleepovers. But the leader needs to be seen as a person first and a boss second. He/she should see their employees as people first and then as employees.

Commitment is huge to a team builder. They are committed to the company's objective, and they expect everyone else to be onboard as well. That works both ways – both professionally and personally. When the team knows their leader is committed to the company and to them, it is easy for them to commit their time, effort, energy and talent to the company and to the boss.

Team builders broadcast and promote an "us" mentality instead of "me vs. you". We are all on the same team, pulling together to win. We all have to row together if we want to beat the competition. We can't afford to be split into factions and indulge in in-fighting.

A yelling match broke out between two managers during a staff meeting. A third manager jumped to his feet, slammed a fist onto the desk, pointed out the window and yelled, "Hey! The (expletive deleted) enemy is out there, not in here!"

Team builders realize the importance of getting others to contribute. Finding the skill set you need and deploying them wisely is not just good business; it is smart tactics and strategy and why you're the boss.

Finally, team builders not only find and deploy smart, talented people, they also know how to motivate others to contribute thereby assuring success for all. When you can recognize, deploy and harness team talent and energy, you tend to succeed. Every coach that has ever won a championship knows that. It is kind of like a great recipe: put all the right parts in, mix them well and out comes something magnificent.

Team Killers

Team killers are quite the opposite of team builders.

Unfortunately, when I have spoken with people about their employment, I most often hear they work for team killers instead of team builders. If team killers can work their way into positions of leadership, they can effectively gum up and even kill off great plans by their ineptitude alone.

Team killers tend to put themselves first, and consider everyone else around them as second-rate. This is ego covering up for an insecure personality.

They tend to be strictly task-oriented where relationships mean nothing (or count for very little). That is not always the case. I do not mean to indicate that task-oriented people are selfish and mean. Thank God for task-oriented people! (If it were not for them we would never get anything done.) What I mean is that since team killers do not value interpersonal relationships, they tend to look past your humanity and see you only as a cog in the wheel that must turn so they can make money. Their attitude is: "If the cog is cracked or broken (under performing), don't bother fixing it (counseling, retraining). Just throw it out (terminate employee) and plug another one in its place (hire new talent)."

Team killers often broadcast and promote a "big me-little you" outlook. If you find yourself hearing all about their success and victories and how you fail them and let them down, they are into the "big me-little you" syndrome. They are a classic case study for the superiority complex.

I know of a boss that moved his company into a new building that had no functioning bathrooms. The facilities were in place but the plumbing was not hooked up yet. He ordered the plumbers to set his bathroom up first. He had his vice president announce everyone else had to drive down the street to a fast-food restaurant to use the bathroom until the plumbers could get to them.

Three weeks later, they got to them.

Can you imagine how they felt about their boss?

Team killers belittle and demean others' success while trumpeting their own. They quite often will wonder how others have managed to succeed at all. Sometimes, they suggest if anyone has succeeded beyond them it is only because the others cheated in some way or had special help. They find it hard to believe that anyone is smarter than they are, including their own employees.

I heard a team killer remark once: "He's not smart. If he was smart he'd have his own company like me." He said this in a room filled with employees – none of whom had their own company. Was that a smart thing to blurt out?

Team killers focus on their own success and brag about themselves. This goes back to the insecurity they harbor. They believe that if they don't toot their own horn, it won't get tooted. So they toot it loud and often. Within a matter of hours you will have heard all of their success stories – whether you asked for them or not.

Team killers are not interested in building up people around them. They are committed strictly to their own success (at everyone else's expense). This comes out in a variety of ways. You do not have to be particularly observant to see how they handle others around them.

Team killers see others as a means to attain personal success. Basically, team builders tend to work toward a goal and they want their team to pull with them so they all succeed. Team killers see people as a means to an end. To a team killer, people are stepping stones on their way to success. Whatever they have to do to get what they want they will do it regardless of how it impacts the lives and careers of those around them. They are so incredibly "me" focused they rarely -- if ever -- see "you". And if they do, it is a distorted and strange "you" they see.

Finally, team killers tend to take credit for all the victories while at the same time assigning all the blame for failure to others. A friend of mine worked (briefly) with a team killer who blurted out one Monday morning: "This office would be so much better were not for all of you!"

How many points do you think he scored with that one?

Lead and inspire people. Don't try to manage and manipulate people. Inventories can be managed but people must be led.

~H. Ross Perot

CHAPTER 4

Team Mates Speak Out

Sit in a deli in a business district at lunch time and you can overhear how people feel about their bosses and their jobs. Because of who I am and what I do I frequently get involved in conversations with people about their work, their bosses and their co-workers. Here are some of the things people tend to say when they are referring to the team builder or the team killer they are employed with.

Team builders are often admired and respected by their team-mates. They tend to smile when they speak of them and use glowing terms like:

- "She's great"
- "I love him"
- "He's a great guy"
- "Best boss in the world"
- "I'd do anything for her"

Employees often refer to the understanding and willingness to work with them on a flexible schedule or they will refer to the integrity and honor they see in their boss. Sometimes they compliment their managers on their organizational gifts or diplomatic skills and make comments like: "I'm learning so much from her."

Team killers on the other hand are generally despised and disrespected by their team. Harsh words, frequent criticism and accusations go a long way to damage relationships between bosses and workers. In distilling the various statements and stories told of team killers, the basic underlying complaint seems to be the boss is unwilling to be flexible or reasonable. Team killers tend to be "bottom line" kind of people who only see the profit margin. Nothing else matters.

I read a story once of a boss who called an employee who took a week off when her mother died. He called to say he was sorry her mom had died, and she needed to be back in the office the following Monday or else.

Would you like to work for that guy?

You will usually find high morale and tight unity around a team builder. Their people are inspired and motivated to work hard, work often and win.

Team killers generate low morale, and no (or little) unity. When you see infighting, turf wars, inter-office conflict, you are either seeing a total absence of leadership or else the leader is a team killer. One of the worst cases is when the team killer has a few select employees he/she trusts and works with, and excludes the others from their inner circle. These are the bosses who only go to lunch with certain employees and definitely not with others. Or the boss who calls a staff meeting and only invites certain people on the staff to attend, leaving the others to wonder what's going on.

A production manager had to take on two new customer service representatives when a sister company folded. He had been in competition with them for so long that even after they were onboard, he excluded them from memos and meetings. He called staff meetings once the two reps went to lunch. They would come back to find a meeting had taken place they had not been invited to which affected their jobs.

Have you ever had a boss hold you accountable for a memo you never received?

Team builders tend to attract talented people to them. Their reputation gets around in their industry, and they become known as a boss you would enjoy working with. Team builders act as magnets for talented people who want to excel in their craft. It doesn't necessarily have anything to do with charisma or personal charm. It has to do with how they take on projects, how they handle their team and how they share victory.

Team killers repel talented people. If you are smart enough to be good at something, you are generally smart enough to pick up very quickly on how a team killer will use you to advance his/her own agenda. People who are smart and talented like to succeed, they have dreams and goals they wish to achieve and they want to do fulfilling work that matters. Once they see the rumor-mongering, backbiting, selfish attitude of a team killer, they will lose interest quickly, update their resume and begin a new job search – even if it means taking a cut in pay!

People want to work for team builders because:

- they believe in the builder
- they believe in the cause of the company
- they like the way they are treated at work

They don't *have* to go to work; they *get* to go to work!

Team killers have the opposite effect on their employees. People who have to work around them every day would be willing to go to work for almost anyone else. If they don't believe in the boss and they don't like the way they are being treated, what the company is trying to accomplish will mean nothing to them. Whereas team builders inspire you to work smarter and better, the only thing a team killer will ever inspire you to do is update your resume and seek new employment!

Team builders are willing to sacrifice on behalf of their workers when necessary. . .

The morale of the deputies was sky-high when their sheriff voluntarily took a pay cut after a dismal budget meeting so he would not have to lay anyone off.

A boss encouraged his employees to bring raffle tickets, candy bars and anything else they were trying to sell to raise funds for their kids' baseball, soccer, dance teams. He even sponsored a team and proudly displayed the team photo in the lobby.

One school district superintendent took a cut in pay, asked his administrators to do the same then volunteered his time in the afternoons to teach tutoring classes in the local schools.

Everyone recognizes a giver. When we see them sacrifice, we want to give too. We're inspired to help when we see our superiors doing the same.

Team killers give as little as necessary. Their view of life is "get what you can while you can" and not "give yourself away". Because they grab all the money and glory they can hold for themselves, their employees tend to feel jilted, cheated, overlooked and underpaid. Most complain of not getting the recognition they deserve.

If the leader is a role model then selfishness breeds selfishness among the employees. By the same token, *selflessness* generates a sense of self-sacrifice for the common good and the greater cause.

Team builders inspire their employees to be committed to the mission of the company and to the leaders personally. That commitment holds during economic downturns and financial storms.

Conversely, team killers employ people who may be committed to the cause (mission) but not necessarily to the leader. If there is no or little investment personally in the relationships at work, then there will be little to no investment from the laborers.

Team builders foster imitation. It's always amusing to go into a company and notice the managers' dress and groom themselves in a similar fashion to the CEO. But it follows in action as well as looks. Generous, gracious leaders inspire the same behavior in their followers.

Where there is no vision, the people perish.

~Proverbs 29:18

CHAPTER 5

Are You a Team Builder or a Team Killer?

Inevitably when you study people who build teams and those who tear them down, you wonder:

Which one am I?

Are you the type of person who can build a team that succeeds? Or would you damage people and ruin their chances at success? No one wakes up in the morning and thinks:

"I'm going to go to work today, and screw up as much as I can."

Most team killers don't even know what they are or the damage they're doing. Conversely, most team builders are very much in touch with who they are and what they are doing. The evidence is all around them.

What follows is a simple survey of questions that if you answer truthfully will let you know if you are a team builder or a team killer. Please DO NOT (as a colleague suggested) turn this into a test you give your middle managers and collect the results so you can judge what they are doing. Instead, have your managers read this book, take the test in private, then consult with you regarding what they are and where they need improvement. I would also recommend you ask these questions not only of yourself but also of anyone you plan on promoting and then have their peers read this book and "grade" those candidates with these questions for you. Their insight may prove to be invaluable and will either confirm or negate your plans.

Team Builder

1. Do people request to work on your team or special projects you are involved in? Is it easy for you to recruit others to help you?

2. Do your team mates volunteer to come in early, stay late, work through lunch or willingly give up weekends to help you? Do they appear to enjoy working alongside you?

3. Do your peers wish to associate with you away from the work place? Is there effort on their part to get to know you better away from work?

4. Have any of your team mates offered to room with you when traveling?

5. When their spouses or children come to visit the office do they go out of their way to make sure and introduce their family to you? Do they ever get into conversations about their families with you?

6. Do your partners ask for your advice and opinions on a variety of things? Or is it strictly business-related?

7. Have you had employees change their work habits to match yours (getting in earlier, staying later, etc.)?

8. Do your workers defend you when you come under attack? Or do they remain silent?

9. Has anyone you've worked with asked you how they can help you succeed? Or offered to do anything that would help you complete a task quicker?

10. Do your co-workers brag on their jobs at your company? Do they try to recruit friends and associates to come work with you?

If you answered "yes" to one or two of these questions you may not be as strong a builder as you thought you were. If you answered "yes" to several of these questions you are on the right track to becoming an excellent team builder. If you were able to honestly answer "yes" to all of these questions, congratulations! You are a great example of a team builder.

As I mentioned earlier, team killers don't wake up in the morning wondering how they can ruin everyone's day. Nor do they plan on coming home with a subordinates' rear end on their breath. Most killers are oblivious that they are tearing down morale and ruining the atmosphere of their work place. Team killers probably wouldn't even read this book, and -- if they did -- they certainly wouldn't finish it. Why should they? They know all they need to know, right?

As you read the following questions, understand that team killers are not monsters dedicated to making your daily life miserable. They just have poor people skills, are blind to everyone else's lives and fixated only on making sure they have job security at the end of the day – even if that means firing you in the process. Some are uneducated in how to deal with people. Others are dealing with trouble at home that boils over at work. Others are following a poor role-model they observed. In short, team killers I have worked with and observed tend to be narcissistic, selfish, egotistical, prideful, self-centered, inwardly focused, uneducated and/or fearful. But that doesn't make them evil. Nor does it mean that they cannot change.

Team Killer

1. Do you have a high turnover among your direct reports? Is it hard to recruit strong talent? As far as your personnel goes, does it appear as if you have a revolving door at your firm?

2. Do your team mates only contribute the bare minimum and then go home? If their desks are vacant by 5:05 p.m., you may have a problem with morale.

3. Do they keep all contact with you strictly business-related? Do you ever get into personal conversations with anyone at your office where they open up and share things from their lives with you?

4. Do they help you only when they are asked to do so?

5. Do they offer ideas when asked? Do they tend to stare at the floor, the walls and the ceiling when you ask for suggestions? This does not necessarily mean they are clueless. It may mean they know any suggestion they offer will be criticized so they've given up on helping you.

6. Do they attack you or allow others to do so? If your office workers get emotional and yell, scream and holler at you or if they stand back and let you get ripped to shreds, they are sending a strong message: *I detest you!* Can you read it?

7. Do they criticize decisions you make to your face or behind your back? Disloyalty is one of the reddest flags they can wave. It is the surest indicator that your team is not unified or respectful of its leader. Ask yourself, "Why?"

8. Do your team mates come in late, leave early, take extra-long lunches, and always

have their weekends booked? In other words, they aren't willing to sacrifice on your behalf or the company's behalf. Granted some of this lackluster performance may be the result of a former manager. But now that you are the leader you should be able to influence habits and routines. They should *want* to come in and help out.

9. Are your employees conducting a new job search while working with you? Finding the classifieds circled in the break room trash can or copies of their resumes accidentally left on the printer is a sure sign they are looking elsewhere. Ask yourself, "Why?"

10. Do your co-workers refer anyone to your open positions or recruit anyone to come join your team?

A leader's role is to raise people's aspirations for what they can become, and to release their energies so they will try to get there.

~David R. Gergen

CHAPTER 6

How Team Killers become Team Builders

Contrary to popular opinion, you *can* teach an old dog new tricks. Studying the psychology of humans changing, behavioral scientists have observed that people change:

a. when they are desperate enough to do so (circumstances make us)

b. when they are taught there is a different, better way (education informs us)

c. when they feel secure enough to try something different (love empowers us)

As you have read through this book and reflected on good and bad bosses you have worked for you may think it is impossible for team killers to change and ever be better bosses. But the truth is:

Everyone can change!

Bad bosses can be taught to become better bosses just as surely as good bosses can (through circumstances) degenerate and develop into someone less than they were when you started with them. If you are a manager of a department or a director in your firm and wondering what you can do to improve your competencies, the following information will be helpful.

There are nine keys that you must possess if you want to change from a killer to a builder – or if you have a killer on your squad you need to convert to a builder. Develop these nine keys into their lives (or your own), and they (and you) will have the basic tools necessary to transform into someone productive and helpful instead of being destructive and harmful.

The Nine Keys to Change

Key # 1: There must be a fundamental change in how self and others are viewed.

Key # 2: Convert from "Big Me, Little You" to a "we're in this together" perspective.

Key # 3: Shift from the "king-leader" to a "servant-leader".

Key # 4: Conduct an honest self-appraisal and find out who you really are.

Key # 5: Define what success means to you.

Key # 6: Define what success means to your peers. How does helping *you* benefit *them*?

Key # 7: Work to set others up to win. How can you help them achieve success?

Key # 8: Change the focus to "us" winning, and not just you.

Key # 9: Learn to share power and glory with those around you.

KEY # 1 – A Fundamental Change in How Self and Others are Viewed

It all begins with perspective. How we view ourselves and how we see others impacts how we treat ourselves and how we treat others. If we are taught growing up that people are special and need to be loved and appreciated, we will have that basic outlook when we interact with our peers. If we observe that people are mean or evil and not to be trusted, then we will be very careful in how we interact with others; not trusting them, believing the worst about them, just waiting for them to do us harm.

This is one of the reasons why exposure to the Judeo-Christian ethic is so profound in American society. It shapes and molds a view toward others that is positive, healthy and empowering. As a minister and human resources professional, I have witnessed the positive impact of a Christian leader on a company as opposed to hypocrites or non-religious leaders and how they affect production and team work. Your viewpoint is shaped by and large by your parents or any adult of significant influence in your life growing up. If you are raised by someone who loves and trusts others, you will tend to be a lover and trust others, too. If you were influenced by someone who was angry and mistrustful of others that will tend to be reflected in your outlook when it comes to working with other people.

It is possible to change and develop the necessary skills to building a winning team.

The first step is to see yourself as a leader who is here to help and build others.

You were not put on this Earth to make all the money in the world by creating the largest company and cornering the market on everything. You are here to lead your team toward victory, empowering and teaching them along the way as you go. You are no better than they are and they are no better than you are. They are skilled in areas you are not talented in and vice versa. They are educated and so are you. They know things you don't know and vice versa. The goal of the company should be to achieve success in the market you work in -- and empowering team mates to win as well.

You need to get away from the "I" syndrome (I think, I feel, I believe, I will) and move more toward the "we" mindset (what shall we do, how shall we respond). It's like moving from singles play in tennis where it is you and the opponent across the net to doubles play where it is you and a partner facing two opponents across the net. In order to win in doubles, you and your partner must be in unison on who plays the net and who plays the line, and/or which side of the court you are responsible for. You have to coordinate your efforts to beat your opponents. If you don't work well with others or you don't communicate well with others, you'll lose all your doubles games. In business, you'll be beaten by the competition who read this book and made the necessary changes.

Think in terms of "we", and not in terms of "me".

KEY # 2: Convert from "Big Me, Little You" to a "We're In This Together" Perspective.

It is generally understood that people who have the need to make you feel small are actually compensating internally for their own smallness. In other words, if I have to put you down and make you feel small it is because I feel small and have a desperate need to feel big. So instead of doing big things to prove my worth and show my value as a giant, I just run you down and make sure you know how small and insignificant you are. Somehow, in the mind of some mentally ill people, that makes them feel powerful and important. It just reveals to the rest of us how weak they are internally.

The "Big Me, Little You" mentality says:

I am important and you are not. My work is significant and yours isn't. I will be remembered and you will be forgotten. I have clout and class and you have none. My value is sky-high. I doubt anyone will ever notice you. I beat you because I am better, and beating you makes me better. I am something and you are nothing. My words deserve to be listened to. You have nothing of any significance to say. I am on top because I deserve to be. You are under me because you deserve to be. I am a better person than you are (i.e., smarter, classier, richer, more influential).

  These kinds of statements are some of the most damaging things a person can ever hear, especially if they are a child or someone who struggles with a low self-esteem. They act like a poison to infect the mind of the weak and those who are susceptible. Bosses who project this mindset or who actually voice these words don't deserve to be in charge of anything. Just the presence of these thoughts in a business person's mind is evidence they are unfit for managing others. A spouse who has this mentality will destroy their marriage. A parent who actually feels this way will do more damage than good to their children. If a minister possesses this outlook, their spiritual impact and ability to work well in the church is minimal.
  No one likes to feel insignificant. Team killers must learn to find value in others, and appreciate what they bring to the table -- even if it seems small and unimportant. Remember: the spokes of a wheel are some of the smallest parts of the bike. But they are all needed to assure our forward progress.
  There is no such thing as "Big Me, Little You". Everyone is important, and we all need to

pull together if we are going to win. The person who wants to play "Big Me, Little You" is really playing another game I call "I am Sick but I want You to Feel Bad". If you struggle with this syndrome, you need to find your own true value and then learn to seek out and appreciate the value in others around you.

KEY # 3: Shift from "King-Leader" to "Servant-Leader".

I got this idea from studying how Jesus of Nazareth interacted with his followers in the New Testament of the Holy Bible. He was a king but it was not significant to him to let others know that. He preferred to just do what he came here to do and let other people figure out who he was and what he was capable of. He didn't spend a lot of time talking about himself, and what he could and could not do. He just did. He did a lot. In fact, he outdid everyone around him, and everyone who had come before him. No one to this date has outdone him yet. I like Jesus because he was a doer more than a talker.

Note to those in charge: don't brag about yourself. Just show me what you got.

Jesus had an interesting take on leadership.

Sitting down, Jesus called the Twelve and said, "Anyone who wants to be first must be the very last, and the servant of all." (Mark 9:35)

In Matthew 20: 25-28 it is written:

> *Jesus called them together and said, "You know that the rulers of the Gentiles lord it over them, and their high officials exercise authority over them. Not so with you. Instead, <u>whoever wants to become great among you must be your servant, and whoever wants to be first must be your slave</u>— just as the Son of Man did not come to be served, but to serve, and to give his life as a ransom for many."*

    The concept of the Servant-King basically means the king casts the vision, clarifies it for the followers, finds out what they need in order to succeed and then helps them do so. Your primary function becomes to role model what you need from them, and then help coordinate efforts so your team achieves its goal.
    The King-Leader says: "Here I am. I am here to win. You all are here to make sure I win."
    The Servant-Leader says: "Here we are. We are here to win. I'm going to help you, and you're going to help me, agreed?"
    You are not in a position of leadership to rule and reign over your subordinates but to help the team achieve success. The goal is not to enrich yourself but to empower your team and thereby "win" through their achievements.
    Think in terms of a winning football coach. He never throws a pass or catches one either. He never rushes for a first down or makes a tackle. Nor does he block a kick or run one back. And yet, if his

team does so consistently, he will be handed a trophy, be given a pay raise, bonuses and may even be recruited to another team for an even larger salary. Why does he get the rewards for what his team does? Because it is recognized that they would not play as well as they do were it not for his coaching and inspiration. By the same token, the Servant-Leader serves the needs of his/her team with the express intention of helping them gain success. The team victory is a natural by-product of your influence and assistance.

KEY # 4: Conduct an Honest Self-Appraisal, and Find Out Who You Really Are.

Have you ever attended a carnival and had a chance to walk through a fun house? Sometimes the floor slopes, the doors open onto walls, and what appear to be windows are actually just drapes over a section of the wall. I like the funny mirror where what is reflected back isn't actually what is real. Because the glass is bent slightly, you either come out looking extremely fat and short or very tall and skinny. That's the way it is sometimes when we try to look at our own lives. Many people tend to only focus on what is wrong with them, and assume it is painfully obvious to everyone. Other people downplay their negatives, and play up the positives of their lives so vividly it appears as if they have no problems at all.

It is hard for us to see where we are failing others. Asking ourselves is fruitless. So is asking friends. They generally tend to tell you what you want to hear. It is best to speak with a counselor or minister, someone who has been trained to work with people and who can afford to be honest with you. Taking surveys and completing questionnaires is okay but the reliability of the final score is based on how honest you were in answering the questions.

It is vital that you understand what makes you tick, what appeals to you, what doesn't and -- perhaps most importantly -- why. The type of department or division you operate will tend to take on your characteristics for better or for worse. That is why it is so important you know who you are and how you operate best.

One of the most painful experiences I ever went through was when two separate friends divided by six years who never knew each other both told me I was selfish and controlling. When the first one told me, I brushed it off as someone who was misinformed and ignorant. But when it happened again the second time, I had to stop and ask myself: *are they seeing something in me I am blind to?* It led to some private counseling sessions which revealed they were both right – I *was* selfish and controlling. That forced me to examine my motives, and deal with what was influencing me to act that way. Those discussions led me to forgiving some people in my past who had controlled me and who -- as a result -- had predisposed me into becoming a controlling personality.

Once you discover your strengths and weaknesses, you are more balanced in your approach toward judging yourself and others. You realize everyone has strengths and weaknesses, and **the key to obtaining harmony and unity is interacting with others in a positive way which plays to their strengths.**

KEY # 5: Define What Success Means to You.

While we are on this journey of self-discovery in our effort to explore the nine keys to transforming from being a team killer into a team builder we need to look at what the meaning of success means to you.

If you were to ask 100 people what success means to them you might be surprised to find that success means different things to different people.

Wealthy and middle-class people in the United States or most Western nations might define success as having plenty of money. For them, if there is enough money to pay all the bills, invest in the future, put some in savings and still have enough to go on vacation then they would probably see themselves as successful people.

For poor people, success might be defined as getting and keeping a job that pays a decent wage. For them, life is more about surviving rather than thriving.

For people who live in third-world countries, having enough to eat and clothes to wear is considered success. Avoiding arrest by crooked cops wanting a bribe is a victory.

I heard a minister say once, "Success is knowing God's will and doing it."

I asked an elderly man once if he saw himself as a success. He said, "I married my wife over 40 years ago, and have always been faithful. My children love and respect us. So, yes, I am successful."

No mention of money, clout, prestige or influence. He didn't live in a large home either, and had retired on a modest income. He taught me that **how people define success is based upon what they see as important in life**.

For some, staying married and having children who love and respect you means you won. For others, it's a big house and nice clothes with an expensive car and elaborate parties.

How do you define success? Is it a certain dollar amount? As in: "Once my net worth is equal to $ _____ then I'll be successful"?

If you have the most attractive spouse does that mean you win? How do you define success? Does success for you mean you're the boss? If you get a gold pin or a wristwatch or a Salesman of the Year trophy does that mean you are a success?

Allow me to pose an idea that I got from studying the life of the greatest leader (and team builder) I have ever read about: Jesus. Suppose I said: *"Success means empowering those around you to become all they are meant to be, and reaping the benefits of their success back into your own life"?*

Think about it.

KEY # 6: Define What Success Means to Your Peers. How Does Joining YOU Benefit THEM?

This is a follow-up question to Key # 5: "Define what success means to you."

Realizing that achieving your dream is a group effort, we must therefore advance to Key # 6: "Define What Success means to Your Peers." As stated in the last section, success means different things to different people. How you define success may not be what your co-workers see as success.

For instance, I had a chance to do some short-term work with a small but growing company. They were making lots of money really fast. You would think morale would have been sky-high due to the generous profit-sharing plan the owner had installed. Instead, there was lots of fighting and adversity between the different department managers. I couldn't believe it. This was a team that was winning on the field, beating out all of their competition but in the dugout, it was chaos. People were stressing out, taking pills, seeing counselors, having fights, storming out, etc. It was amazing! They were the best at what they did and they were cleaning up financially but they hated one another. One manager had a heart attack. Another lady overdosed at home. A manager slammed his vehicle into several other cars in the parking lot after a yelling match in a board meeting.

I had a telephone conversation with one of the administrative assistants later who confided: "I'm never going back to work there. I don't care how much money they offer me."

Obviously success does not always mean a big paycheck. Your peers may feel like having job security equals success. Perhaps it's having the corner office with the nice view. Maybe success for some means working close to home or working from home. Success may mean a Porsche to you but for someone else you work with it might mean just having a car that is reliable that they can afford.

The bottom line is **you need to know your people well enough to know what matters to them.**

While mentioning some of your past successes and personal assets may impress some, it will not impress everyone. As a leader who wishes to have followers, you need to know your people. What do they like? What do they not like? What motivates them? What are they striving for? Can you help them achieve it?

Tied into that question is this one: *how can joining you and your team benefit them?*

Just for kicks, let's throw money out of the equation. It is too easy to answer, "It will benefit them because I will pay them well, and share my profits with them." Let's pretend for a moment that anywhere they go to work they can make the kind of money you are offering, and there are other profit-sharing programs out there that equal or surpass yours.

Now, what do you have to offer that would make them want to come work for you? This is where you develop some intangibles that can make your opportunity irresistible. This is where you have to know what motivates people besides money. Lone Rangers and team killers can't get past this barrier. All they can think of is either making more money or the glory of working with them. It takes some smarts to get to know your people, find out what makes them tick and find a way to motivate them to want to do their best for you by offering them some of what they want in life. When you start thinking in these terms you are developing into a team builder.

KEY # 7: Set Others Up To Win. How Can You Help Them Achieve Success?

By now, you probably see a pattern between team builders and team killers. It is as blatant as serving yourself or serving others. People would rather work with a selfless person instead of a selfish one. A casual glance at these keys to becoming a team builder will reveal how they all interact and overlap one another.

If you've killed a few teams and decide to change how you view yourself and others, you'll soon realize the "Big Me, Little You" perspective is destructive to success and unity. The "Big Me, Little You" ideology springs from the King-Leader viewpoint ("I'm the Boss of all Bosses"). In forsaking that thought, you move toward the Servant-Leader philosophy ("I am here to help you win"). This usually makes us do some inner thinking and conduct a personal inventory to discover who we are, why we think the way we do, how it benefits us and our unit and how it fails us. That will make you ultimately redefine what success means to you, and in time what success means to others.

As a Servant-Leader, you will appreciate what other workers bring to the table. You will move from a "me" mentality to an "us" mentality. This improves marriages, empowers church congregations, emboldens your family and strengthens your relationships.

The Servant-Leader looks for ways to set other people up for success. How can you help them win? What do they need to succeed? How can you help them find that piece? Do you know people you need to introduce them to? Is there something in your library that would help them? You slowly transform from a "What can I get out of them?" mindset to a "What can I give them to help them win?" mindset.

I worked with a business owner named Dave. He had an assistant named Paula who loved her boss. I didn't see Paula much but Dave couldn't say enough nice things about her. Nor could she quit bragging on him. I probed a little and discovered she worked from home. But through her cell phone and her laptop with internet service, Paula was able to get everything done for Dave just as efficiently as if she had been there at the office with him.

She told me she had approached him the previous year, and told him:

(a) she was pregnant again, and wanted to spend more time at home with her husband and child, and

(b) the commute was killing her (almost an hour each way).

Paula told Dave she liked working for him, and wanted to keep doing so. She wondered if he might be willing to try a "work from home" set-up for three months.

"If it is too difficult to manage, I'll come back to the office," she promised.

Dave was doubtful they could pull it off. But he liked Paula's work ethic and drive. So he decided to give it a 90-day trial, then they would honestly discuss the pros and cons, and decide whether they needed to end the experiment or keep it going.

The plan worked! Through the internet, a cell phone, and a fax machine, she was able to perform all the paper work and purchases the boss needed. The receptionist became more involved working with the boss, and Paula and her family loved the new schedule.

This is an example of a Servant-Leader who rearranged his thinking to help his subordinate achieve her dream. It was a win-win for them both, and cemented her loyalty to him even more so when he made time for her husband and children.

One more story of how a boss set up someone to achieve success:

Tony was a production assistant in the warehouse but wanted to be in a leadership role. He approached his supervisor, Dan about it since Dan was about to go on vacation. Tony thought this would be an excellent opportunity for him to step up and show what he could do. They talked it over with Ed, the warehouse manager. Ed had his doubts but decided to give Tony his shot.

Dan went on vacation. Tony started running things. Ed made several appearances and reassured Tony he was there for him if he needed him. Monday and Tuesday things went fine. Wednesday there was a back-up that delayed orders getting out. Thursday there was a miscommunication that jammed the line some more. Friday a few machines broke down and needed servicing which made everyone have to work late. They got paid more but they also got home late, and the slow down cost the company thousands of dollars.

Dan got back on Monday and Ed gave Tony an honest appraisal – which was not very flattering. He was kind though and left Tony with his dignity intact. Tony appreciated the opportunity and Ed's honesty, and had a newfound appreciation for Dan, his supervisor.

This isn't necessarily a tale of victory. But it is real-life and shows that sometimes when we try and help people win, they fail. How we handle their failure can determine whether they stay with us or not. Some people you can set up to win and they will soar. Others you can try to help and they will fall. If they crash, try to help them not to burn. (If they do burn, help them put the fire out and reassure them the scorched look is in season.) You have to be wise in how you handle company assets but I think it is better to let people try and fail than to shut them down and not ever try a new way. It is better to have it said of you "He/she gave me a chance" than to have it said of you, "No one ever got anywhere with them."

KEY# 8: Change The Focus To "Us" Winning, And Not Just You.

When I was in high school I loved playing tennis. But I didn't play doubles. I didn't like doubles. Doubles meant I had to depend on someone else to win. I didn't want to depend on anyone. I wanted to depend only on me. I was sure of my abilities and felt confident if it all came down to me and my racket I would win the game. I won a lot and lost some, too. But I often reflect back to my attitude in high school when I meet King-Leaders or insecure team killers who don't trust anyone but themselves.

In reality there is only so much you can accomplish by yourself. Even activities you would perceive as being a lonely occupation like writing a book takes others to help you. As I sit and type these words on my word processor, I am aware of the fact that without the invention of the computer and MS Word I would have to write this on a tablet with a pen. I am also dependent on the US postal service to get my proposed manuscript to a publisher. I need the publisher to agree to publish my book. I am a writer. I know next to nothing about how to go about marketing and selling my book. I am dependent on the experts at the publishing company to make this happen for me. And finally, I am dependent on you, the consumer to pick up my book, read the front and back covers, maybe scan the table of contents and then decide if it is something interesting enough for you to sit down and actually read.

So you can see, though writing would appear to be a one-man (or one-woman) show, in reality it takes a lot of people all doing their jobs well to get ideas I have in my mind into your hands to read.

The same can be said of a great tennis player. She may practice every day and play well in every tournament, but ultimately she is not in this alone – even if she is the single's champion of the world. Someone made her racket. Someone made her shoes. Someone taught her how to play. Someone still coaches her every day. Someone has to make her travel arrangements to the various tournaments. She needs an accountant to manage her money, a lawyer to handle her contracts and a publicist to keep her name and picture in the press.

None of us are an island. All of us are interconnected. Therefore, none of us can truthfully say we are self-made. It only follows that if we manage to succeed in anything we had help doing it, and if we did, then everyone deserves the credit. Team killers like taking all the credit for anything done well because they are weak and insecure and feel the need to brag and boast even when they've no right to. Team builders on the other hand are strong and secure with who they are and what they can do. They are also smart enough to realize that it takes a team to win and that teams deserve recognition.

Team builders develop and adopt an "us" mentality. Each win is a team win. No one goes it alone because we all know you can't go very far alone. When you add the talents of several people who are disciplined and focused and add synergy to their effort, they become an unstoppable force. Give them a goal and motivate them to win – not just through gigantic paychecks but by offering them a piece of what they really are striving for – and they will move Heaven and Earth to succeed.

KEY # 9: Learn to Share Power with Those Around You.

Ask yourself a question:

Why do I have to be the king?

Why is it so important to you that people look up to you and admire you? Find the true answer to that question, and you'll understand the difference between security and insecurity.

There were two boys in grammar school who were secretly given cookies by their teacher. One of them bragged about the cookies he had. He held them out for the other students to see, waving them in their faces, teasing and taunting them, grinning because he had them and they did not. He delighted in chewing them slowly while the other students looked on jealously.

The second boy gave one to a friend and halved another with a girl he liked. Over the course of one-half hour, he shared two more with other boys and halved another with the same girl.

Later that day, the teacher talked about sharing and being generous. She handed out play money to all of the children, and asked them to share their money with whomever they pleased.

The money got spread around pretty evenly -- except for two kids. The generous cookie giver got a little more than the others got, and the stingy teaser got hardly any at all.

Lesson learned?

When you share the wealth your value goes up and others are more likely to share with you. Be stingy with what you have, and you may end up broke and alone.

In Galatians 6:7 the Apostle Paul wrote:

"Do not be deceived: God cannot be mocked. A man reaps what he sows."

If we sow in kindness and generosity, we will reap the same back into our own life. If we sow cruelty, jealousy and selfishness, that is what returns to us.

If we get out of life what we sow into it then it makes sense to be generous with others.

The key to successfully transforming from being a team killer to a team builder begins with a change in you. Once your outlook switches from being me-focused to other-focused you can begin building up other people. Say to them what you would like said of you. Do for them what you would like for them to do for you. In making them powerful and enabling them to go forward, you'll attract folks to you who want to work with you.
Why?
Because you'll be seen as a dream maker.

Help your colleagues' dreams come true, and yours will too.

Builders are not born. They are made. They are forged in the fire of relationships. Builders have learned that when I help you win, the favor will be returned to me. If you do not or cannot return it, someone else will. The more I give away, the more I will be given to give away. I don't have to worry about someone taking my job if I am doing it well. Even if it appears that someone has, I'll just find a new and better one somewhere else. I don't fear training or promoting you. I look forward to it.

Builders are good at passing on the knowledge necessary to ascend and also the heart that goes with it.

Have a generous heart.

A young engineer interviewed for his first job with a large company. The manager was a senior engineer, heading the department the young man might be working in.

He said: "You've never worked for a company this size before. Why should we hire you?"

The young man thought a moment and answered: "Sir, it's true I've never worked for a big company before. But I'm not asking you for anything but a chance. Someone gave you a chance once. Now I'm asking you to give me one. Let me prove what I can do."

He was hired, and did quite well.

Someone has been kind to you in the past. Be kind to those around you and to others in your future. People have helped you. Now it is your turn to help others.

Success isn't about what title you bear or how much money you make. It's about how much you pour into other people's lives. It's about giving yourself away.

At the end of your life, people won't remember how much you died with or your estimated worth. They'll either speak of how shallow and cruel you were or how kind and pleasant you were. Your attitude and actions will decide that.

If your actions inspire others to dream more, learn more, do more and become more, you are a leader.

~John Quincy Adams

About the Author

As a minister involved in church work for over 20 years, Steven Galindo has had lots of experience building teams on a volunteer basis.

As a Human Resources professional for 14 years, he has developed teamwork, harmony and unity out of chaotic, angry workplace environments.

He is a pastor, teacher, counselor, singer and author. A native Houstonian, he and his wife, Robyn live in Joplin, Missouri.

Mr. Galindo is available for conferences, group and individual training as well as private counseling sessions.

You may write him at:
stevengalindo61@gmail.com

Or visit his website at:
www.galindosbooks.com

More books by Steven Galindo follow . . .

The Healing Power of Forgiveness

    Are you troubled by memories filled with shame and regret? Do you struggle with forgiving others for past hurts? Do you feel remorse and need to be forgiven?

    In The Healing Power of Forgiveness, pastor and author Steven Galindo discusses how to forgive others, how to forgive yourself and how to forgive God as well as how to ask for and receive forgiveness, and how to release the past so you can embrace your future.

    This is an excellent reference for therapists, counselors and anyone suffering inner pain and needing release. Walk out of bondage and into freedom. Release your pain and unlock your joy!

Visit www.galindosbooks.com to purchase your copy now!

From a Pit to a Palace, From Prisoner to Prince: Lessons Learned from the Life of Joseph

Follow pastor and author Steven Galindo as he takes an enlightening journey through the life of Joseph, the ancient Hebrew patriarch. Along the way, you'll learn some important lessons about dreaming God's dreams, finding your spiritual gifts, defining the true meaning of success and understanding your place in the Kingdom of God.

Each chapter is followed with important Lessons Learned as well as Questions to Discuss, making it ideal for small group study or one-on-one counseling.

The Gift My Father Gave Me

At 17, Matthew discovers he is adopted. He and his Dad board a bus to cross Texas meet his biological father, the mysterious *Tio* Antonio.

Along the way we learn the story of his adoption, and see Matthew receive two gifts -- wealth from Tio Antonio, and an even more valuable one from his father.

This is a novel about integrity. In it we learn what makes us rich is not what we have but who we are.

Go to www.galindosbooks.com to buy your copy now!

Healing Mercy, Healing Faith, Healing Grace and Healing Power

Four devotionals designed to inspire and encourage those struggling with illness. Each book offers 30 healing scriptures and a short commentary that will uplift and inform doctors, nurses, ministers, counselors and loved ones of the healing power of God.

Despite what some cynics and critics may think, God is still in the healing business, and He has a word of healing for you and your family members.

A Prescription for Peace

The world is full of trials and difficulties. It is easy to lose your peace of mind and give in to worry, fear, doubt and anxiety.

A Prescription for Peace is medicine from the Bible that restores tranquility to the troubled soul. Each page of this 30-page devotional offers a scripture, a commentary and a prayer designed to calm your nerves, encourage your heart and develop your peace of mind.

This is a wonderful resource for counselors, pastors and chaplains working with struggling believers.

Get your copy at: www.galindosbooks.com.

The Blood and the Cross

    Once you understand the power resident in the blood of Jesus and the meaning of the cross of Calvary you can live a victorious, overcoming life as a Christian believer.

    In The Blood and the Cross, pastor and author Steven Galindo shares seven messages on the power found in the blood of Jesus and the cross of Calvary. Touching on the history of blood sacrifice and explaining the Roman execution style of crucifixion, you will see why Christ had to die, and what His death and resurrection means for you today. Special emphasis is placed on the power of the cross and the blood to heal and change us. It will shift your perception of God forever.

Greeting and Ushering

First impressionas are lasting impressions. What people see and experience when they walk into your church foyer will either impress them and draw them in or make them want to visit another church next week.

Greeting and Ushering is a practical guide to ushering and greeting in church services. It differentiates between the two ministries, explains their purposes and coaches you in how to build a vital, well-prepared team who will not only greet and seat visitors but engage them in conversation and service.

Excellent for training new volunteers! A test is included.

Get your copy at: www.galindosbooks.com.

Acknowledgements

Special thanks to Mark Shead at www.leadership501.com/leadership-quotes/316 for the collation and distribution of the leadership quotes.

www.ingramcontent.com/pod-product-compliance
Lightning Source LLC
Chambersburg PA
CBHW051728170526
45167CB00002B/851